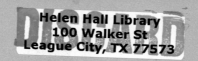

SCHOLASTIC discover more™

planets

By Penelope Arlon
and
Tory Gordon-Harris

How to discover more

Planets is a very simple book to use and enjoy. By knowing a little bit about the way it works, you will have fun reading and discover more.

The pages

Every page is a little bit different, but all of them will give you lots of information, stunning pictures, and great facts.

The introduction tells you what the pages are about.

Labels tell you what you are looking at.

Captions tell you more about the subject.

This symbol means that you can see the subject in the night sky without using a telescope.

Mercury

Mercury is the closest planet to the Sun. That means it's hot—four times hotter than boiling water!

PLANET NUMBER **1**

Mercury is the fir... smallest planet in solar system. It al... has the fastest or...

Solar panel

Sun shade

Magnet

Mariner 10, *like o... space probes, flie... through space without people on board.*

Mariner 10
Mariner 10 was the first space probe to fly to Mercury. It left Earth in 1973 and flew past Mercury three times.

Use the Internet to find out when Mercury will appear brightest in the sky.

YOU CAN SEE

From Earth
Mercury is difficult to see from Earth becau... it is so close to the Su... and gets lost in its lig... It is visible for a few hours after sunset an... before sunrise.

18

Although Mercury's journey around the Sun is the

Digital companion book

Download your free all-new digital book,

Amazing Space Machines

Log on to
www.scholastic.com/discovermore

Enter your unique code:
RCHHFXD774W9

Discover amazing space machines

This box lets you know each planet's position in the solar system.

Small text gives you interesting facts about the pictures.

Look up a favorite subject in the contents.

ky planet

ury is one of the planets. It is ed in huge dents, craters. Craters ade by big rocks, asteroids, that into it.

Mercury has a huge crater on it called the Caloris Basin. It is 808 miles (1,300 kilometers) wide.

PLANET DATA
Average distance from the Sun:
37 million miles
(60 million km)

Length of day:
59 Earth days
Length of year:
88 Earth days

Name: Mercury was named after the winged god because it is fast.

If you stood on Mercury, the Sun would look **2½** times bigger than it does on Earth.

Moons: 0

HE **HOTTEST** SURFACE EMPERATURE ON MERCURY IS **801°F** (427°C).

est, Mercury is not the fastest-rotating planet. 19

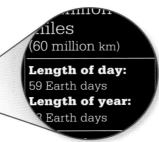

...illion ...iles
(60 million km)

Length of day:
59 Earth days
Length of year:
...3 Earth days

The data boxes give vital information and statistics for every planet.

Look up or learn new words in the glossary.

Look up a word in the index and find which page it's on.

▶▶▶ **Find out more**
This takes you to another page with related information.

The bottom line gives bite-size facts and asks you questions.

Click the pop-ups to find out even more

Encyclopedia entries packed with facts

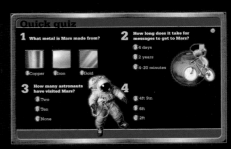

Fun space quizzes

Consultant: Dr. Craig Underwood, BSc, PGCE, PhD, FBIS, MIEEE
Literacy Consultant: Jane E. Mekkelsen, Literacy & Learning Connections LLC
Art Director: Bryn Walls
Designer: Ali Scrivens
Managing Editor: Miranda Smith
US Editor: Beth Sutinis
Cover Designer: Natalie Godwin
DTP: John Goldsmid, Sunita Gahir
Visual Content Editor: Diane Allford-Trotman
Executive Director of Photography, Scholastic: Steve Diamond

Library of Congress Cataloging-in-Publication Data Available

ISBN 978-0-545-33028-2

10 9 8 7 6 5 4 3 2 1   12 13 14 15 16

Printed in Singapore   46
First edition, January 2012

Contents

Planets

A planet is a round object that orbits, or circles around, a star and reflects light from that star. A planet is either rocky or made up of gases.

Our planet family

There are eight primary planets that orbit our star—the Sun. Our planet, Earth, is one of these planets.

Planet journeys

For thousands of years, people watched the stars, which move across the sky like a giant floating map. Some of these stars seemed to move differently—that's because they are actually planets, not stars.

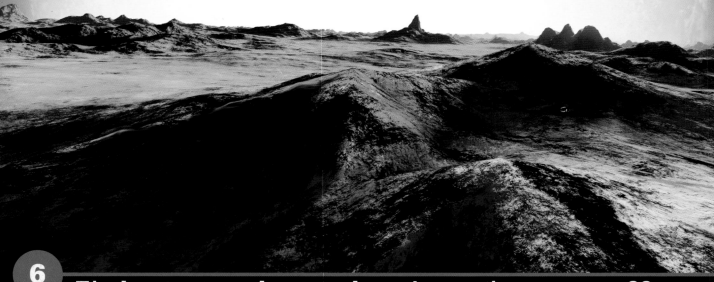

All planets are round. They are made round by a force called gravity.

Find out more about a planet's gravity on page 22.

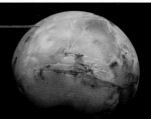

Mars is made of rock and metal, just like Earth.

Rocky planets

Some planets in our solar system are made of rock, metal, or both. They are hard enough to stand on.

The planet Uranus is made of gas and liquid.

Gas giants

Some planets in our solar system are made of gas or liquid. They are very big. You couldn't stand on these planets.

Pluto was once thought to be a primary planet.

Dwarf planets

Dwarf planets like Pluto are smaller objects that also orbit our Sun. They lie much farther away than the eight primary planets.

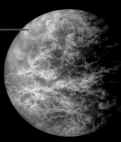

There could be life on distant planets, like this one.

Extrasolar planets

Scientists are now discovering planets in space that circle other stars. More than 500 have been spotted so far.

Moons

Some planets have moons that orbit them. Our planet, Earth, has one moon. Other planets have many more—Jupiter has 63 moons!

Jupiter has four big moons and lots of smaller ones.

Where are we?

The whole of space is called the universe. It is so big that it's difficult to imagine. Earth is one of countless planets in the universe.

The universe

When you look at the stars, you are looking into the universe. Everything you can see is in the universe.

Our place in the sky

Although we don't know exactly how big the universe is, we do know what is around us. Let's start at our home and zoom out to take a look.

planet
Our planet is the Earth. It is the third planet from our Sun.

home
This is a picture of a house taken from the air.

town
Zoom out farther into the sky and we can see a town with lots of houses.

state
Zoom out again to see that the town is in a state, where millions of people live.

country
Zoom out even farther to see that the state is part of a huge country on Earth.

Find out more about galaxies on page 51.

The universe is still growing outward. We know this

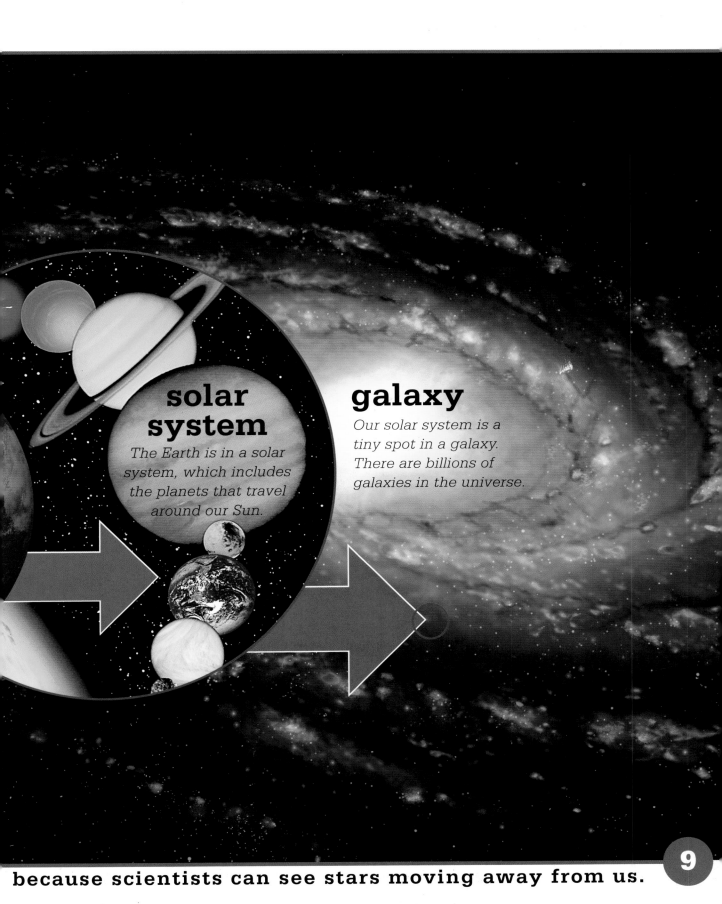

solar system

The Earth is in a solar system, which includes the planets that travel around our Sun.

galaxy

Our solar system is a tiny spot in a galaxy. There are billions of galaxies in the universe.

because scientists can see stars moving away from us.

The solar system

The Sun is at the center of our solar system. Millions of objects travel around it. The biggest objects are the eight primary planets. Each planet rotates as it travels around the Sun.

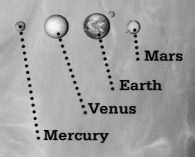

Mars

Earth

Venus

Mercury

.Jupiter

Mercury
Mercury is the closest planet to the Sun. It is very hot on Mercury.

Venus
Venus is a similar size to Earth but it is surrounded by poisonous clouds.

Earth
Earth is the third planet from the Sun and so far it is the only planet known to have life.

Mars
Mars is known as the red planet. Space probes have landed on Mars.

Find out how far the planets are from

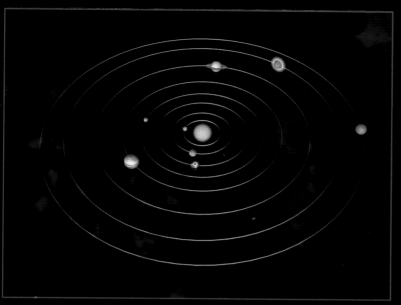

Planet paths

All eight primary planets travel around the Sun in almost perfect circles, or orbits. The Sun's gravity keeps all the planets near it like a giant magnet, keeping them from drifting away into space.

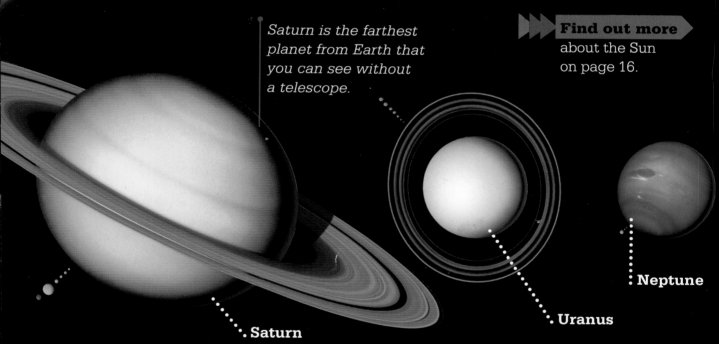

Saturn is the farthest planet from Earth that you can see without a telescope.

Find out more about the Sun on page 16.

Neptune

Uranus

Saturn

Jupiter
Jupiter is the biggest planet in our solar system. It is a giant gas ball.

Saturn
Saturn has the largest and most spectacular rings around it.

Uranus
Uranus is the seventh planet from the Sun. It has rings, but they are very faint.

Neptune
Neptune is the farthest planet from the Sun. It is very chilly and dark on Neptune.

Gods in the sky

Mercury was named after the messenger of the gods.

More than 2,000 years ago the Romans named the planets after their gods. We still use some of these names today.

Mars was named after the Roman god of war because it is red, like blood.

Venus was the Roman goddess of love.

The name Earth is from the Anglo-Saxon word erda, meaning "soil."

MERCURY

DIAMETER
3,032 miles
(4,880 kilometers)

FACT
Mercury is the smallest planet in our solar system.

MADE OF
Rock

MOONS
0

VENUS

DIAMETER
7,520 miles
(12,102 kilometers)

FACT
Venus is the hottest planet in our solar system.

MADE OF
Rock

MOONS
0

EARTH

DIAMETER
7,926 miles
(12,755 kilometers)

FACT
Earth is the largest of the rocky planets in our solar system.

MADE OF
Rock

MOONS
1

MARS

DIAMETER
4,222 miles
(6,795 kilometers)

FACT
The planet Mars has seasons, just as Earth does.

MADE OF
Rock

MOONS
2

In Ancient Greek times, people invented symbols for

Jupiter was the king of the Roman gods— a good name for the largest planet in our solar system.

Saturn was the father of Jupiter. Saturn was the farthest planet that the Romans could see in the sky.

Uranus was not known in ancient times. It was named after a Greek god in 1781.

Neptune was named in modern times, after the Roman god of the sea.

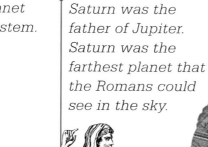

JUPITER

DIAMETER
88,846 miles
(142,984 kilometers)

FACT
Jupiter is the fastest-spinning planet in our solar system.

MADE OF
Gas and liquid

MOONS
63

SATURN

DIAMETER
74,900 miles
(120,540 kilometers)

FACT
Saturn is so light that it would float on water!

MADE OF
Gas and liquid

MOONS
62

URANUS

DIAMETER
31,763 miles
(51,118 kilometers)

FACT
From Earth, you can see Uranus only through a telescope.

MADE OF
Gas and liquid

MOONS
27

NEPTUNE

DIAMETER
30,755 miles
(49,495 kilometers)

FACT
Neptune is the windiest planet in the solar system.

MADE OF
Gas and liquid

MOONS
13

the planets, such as ☿ for Mercury.

Space exploration

Humans started to explore space in the 1950s. Before then, we could only gaze at the night sky.

......V2

1543
Nicolaus Copernicus realizes that the Sun stays still and the planets move around it.

1781

Sir William Herschel announces the discovery of Uranus on March 13, 1781.

1942
The German V2 rocket is the first to exit the Earth's atmosphere.

1957
The Soviet Union sends the first animal into space. It is a dog named Laika.

1610
Galileo Galilei invents the telescope and discovers that Jupiter has moons.

1846
An eighth planet is discovered in our solar system—Neptune.

1959
The first photo of Earth is taken from space.

Years ago . . .
Thousands of years ago people looked up at the stars and planets at night. They examined them closely and named them.

Sputnik 1

YOU CAN SEE
Look out for this symbol. It shows something you can spot in the night sky.

1957
The Soviet Union launches the first satellite, Sputnik 1, into space.

Find out more about the moon walk on page 26.

1981

The first space shuttle, Columbia, *flies into space and back again.*

1995

The Galileo space probe orbits Jupiter for the first time.

1961

Yuri Gagarin of the Soviet Union is the first human to fly into space.

1986

People live in space for the first time, on the Russian space station Mir.

2000

The ISS (International Space Station) is launched.

2001

Dennis Tito pays millions of dollars to take a trip into space as the first space tourist.

1969

The world watches as Neil Armstrong is the first human to step onto the Moon.

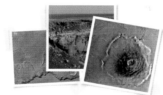

1976

NASA collects the first photos and soil samples from the surface of Mars.

1990

The Hubble Space Telescope is launched and gives the world a whole new view of space.

???

What is our future in space? Vacations in space, or a hotel on the Moon, perhaps?

Hubble Space Telescope

Our Sun

The Sun that lights our world is actually a star. It is a superhot ball of fiery gas that is very, very big. It gives us heat and light.

ONE MILLION EARTHS could fit inside OUR SUN.

THE DIAMETER OF THE SUN IS 109 TIMES BIGGER THAN EARTH'S DIAMETER.

Solar flares

The Sun throws out waves of heat called solar flares. If they travel close to Earth, they cause power outages. A flare cut off the telegraph wires 150 years ago. Imagine what it could do to our computers today!

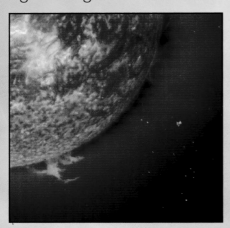

An enormous solar flare shoots out from our Sun.

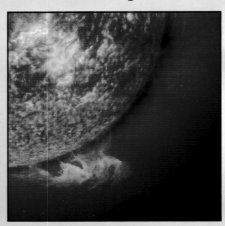

It travels toward Earth like a heat storm.

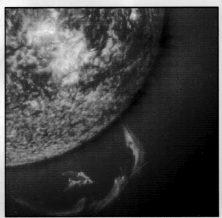

It breaks up in space before it reaches the Earth.

The Sun is about 93 million miles (150 million km) from

MEDIUM STAR
Our Sun is only a medium-size star, even though it looks big to us. Some stars are much bigger.

An adult is the size of the Sun.

 The marble is the Earth.

MARBLE EXPERIMENT
Walk a marble 100 steps away from an adult. That is how far Earth is from the Sun, and how much bigger the Sun is than Earth.

Find out more about comets on page 47.

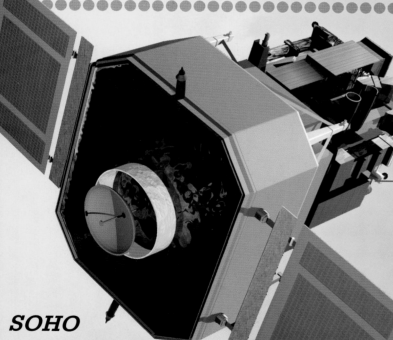

SOHO orbits the Sun and is about 1 million miles (1.5 million kilometers) closer to the Sun than Earth is.

SOHO
The space probe SOHO was sent into space in 1995 to study the Sun. It sends back images and information about the Sun's temperature and winds.

While studying the Sun, SOHO has discovered 2,000 comets!

Earth. It takes eight minutes for sunlight to reach us.

Mercury

Mercury is the closest planet to the Sun. That means it's hot—four times hotter than boiling water!

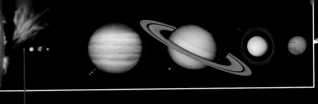

Mercury is the first and smallest planet in our solar system. It also has the fastest orbit.

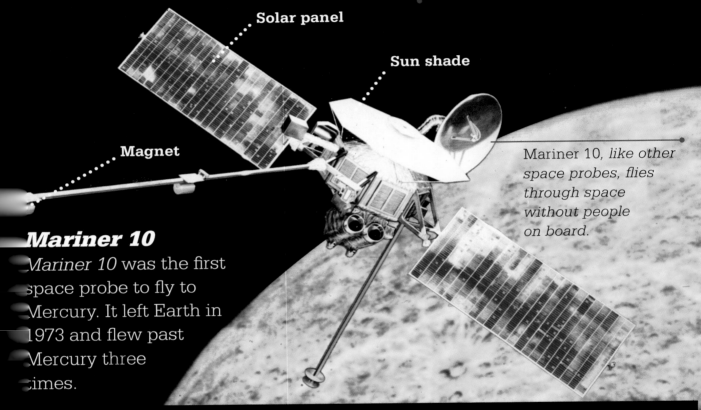

Solar panel

Sun shade

Magnet

Mariner 10, like other space probes, flies through space without people on board.

Mariner 10

Mariner 10 was the first space probe to fly to Mercury. It left Earth in 1973 and flew past Mercury three times.

Use the Internet to find out when Mercury will appear brightest in the sky.

YOU CAN SEE

From Earth

Mercury is difficult to see from Earth because it is so close to the Sun and gets lost in its light. It is visible for a few hours after sunset and before sunrise.

Although Mercury's journey around the Sun is the

Rocky planet

Mercury is one of the rocky planets. It is covered in huge dents, called craters. Craters are made by big rocks, called asteroids, that crash into it.

Mercury has a huge crater on it called the Caloris Basin. It is 808 miles (1,300 kilometers) wide.

THE **HOTTEST** SURFACE TEMPERATURE ON **MERCURY** IS **801°F** (427°C).

PLANET DATA	
Average distance from the Sun: 37 million miles (60 million km)	
Length of day: 59 Earth days	
Length of year: 88 Earth days	
Name: Mercury was named after the winged god because it is fast.	
If you stood on Mercury, the Sun would look **2½** times bigger than it does on Earth.	
Moons: 0	

fastest. Mercury is not the fastest-rotating planet.

Venus

Venus is known as Earth's twin as it is a similar size and is made of similar rock.

2

Venus is the second planet from the Sun, and the planet that is nearest to Earth.

Cloudy days

Venus has a rocky landscape and yellow clouds. The clouds are so thick that sunlight never reaches the surface. Every day is cloudy on Venus.

YOU CAN SEE

Venus is easy to spot in the starry sky. Other than the Moon, it is the brightest natural object.

Find out more
about space probes on page 38.

20

A day is one complete rotation of a planet. Earth's day i

The journey of the *Magellan* space probe

1 Blast off
In 1989, the shuttle *Atlantis* launched the *Magellan* space probe on a journey to Venus.

2 To work
A year later, the probe arrived and spent four years orbiting Venus and sending back data.

3 The end
In 1994, *Magellan* plunged into Venus's atmosphere, and the corrosive air destroyed it.

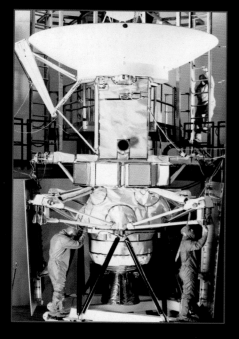

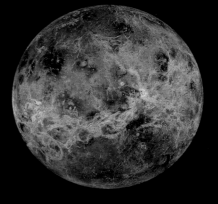

PLANET DATA
Average distance from the Sun:
67 million miles (107 million km)
Length of day: 243 Earth days
Length of year: 225 Earth days

Name: Venus was the Roman goddess of love.

Moons: 0

Burning hot
Venus is farther from the Sun than Mercury, yet it is hotter at 900°F (480°C). Venus rotates slowly, so the Sun heats it for months at a time without cooling nights. The clouds keep the heat in, so it stays very hot.

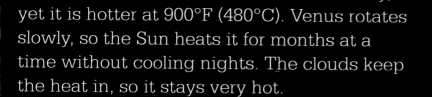

24 hours. Venus's day lasts for 243 Earth days!

Our planet, Earth, is the only one in our solar system known to have oceans and life. That makes our planet very special indeed.

3

The third planet from the Sun is our own planet Earth.

Earth has only one moon.

Atmosphere

Our planet is surrounded by a thick layer of gases, called the atmosphere, which is held in place by gravity. It is like a bubble protecting us from the Sun's rays.

Gravity

The Earth tries to pull everything toward its center. This pull is called gravity. Gravity is the reason that things fall to the ground when you drop them, and why we can walk without floating away.

When astronauts go into space, they float around.

It takes a day for the Earth to rotate on itself

Life on Earth

Earth is the only planet we know of that has life on it. Plants and animals need water, the right air, and the perfect temperature to survive. Earth is the ideal place to live.

PLANET DATA

Average distance from the Sun:

93 million miles
(150 million km)

Length of day:
23 hours, 56 minutes

Length of year:
365¼ days

Moons: 1

In the center of the Earth is an iron core where temperatures reach **10,832°F (6,000°C)**—this is as hot as the surface of the Sun.

It takes one year for the Earth to travel around the Sun.

Our Moon

Our Moon is our closest neighbor in space. It revolves around Earth and is the brightest object in the sky at night.

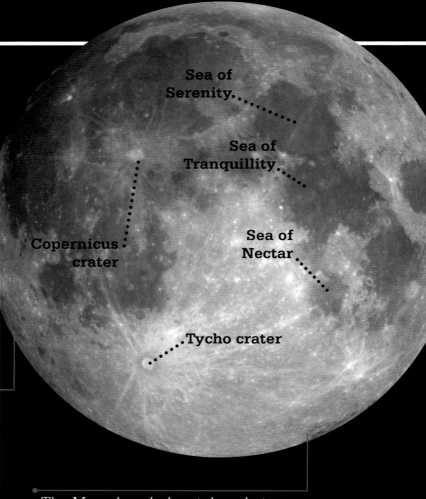

Sea of Serenity

Sea of Tranquillity

Copernicus crater

Sea of Nectar

Tycho crater

The Moon is covered in dents, called craters, where huge rocks, called meteorites, have hit it in the past.

The Moon has dark patches that we call seas, but these are not filled with water, like seas on Earth are.

Moon phases

It takes about 29½ days for a full Moon to become full again.

Changing Moon

Have you ever noticed that the Moon changes shape each day? We see different parts of it depending on how much sunlight shines on it.

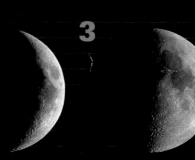

1

2

3

New Moon

Draw the shape of the Moon every night for a month

Eclipse

Sometimes the Moon moves right between the Sun and the Earth. It completely blocks out the light from the Sun for up to eight minutes. This is called an eclipse.

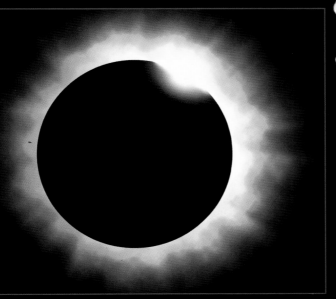

We only ever see one side of the Moon from Earth— the near side. The other half is called the far side.

The changing shapes are called phases.

5
Full Moon

6

7

8

MAN ON THE MOON!

"The *Eagle* has landed"

The Moon landing

It was July 20, 1969, when 600 million people all over the Earth watched their television screens as the small lunar module called *Eagle* touched down on the Moon. It was the first time humans had walked on any surface away from our Earth.

250,000
miles from Earth to the Moon

Buzz Aldrin stands on the surface of the Moon.

The mission diary

JULY 16, 1969

Neil Armstrong, Edwin "Buzz" Aldrin, and Mike Collins blast off on the *Apollo 11* mission.

Ready for takeoff

JULY 20, 1969

After traveling through space for four days, the astronauts arrive at the Moon. Neil Armstrong and Buzz Aldrin strap themselves into the *Eagle* and drop down onto the surface of the Moon. Mike Collins stays in the spacecraft, flying around the Moon.

JULY 20, 02:56 GMT

At 02:56 Greenwich Mean Time, Neil Armstrong steps out of the *Eagle* (below) and puts his left foot down.

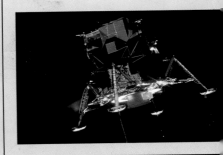

A legacy for the future

The *Eagle* landed on the Sea of Tranquillity.

A footprint left on the Moon by the astronauts.

The astronauts put the American flag into the Moon dust. They also left behind a bag containing a golden olive leaf— a sign of peace—and a silicon disc carrying messages from President Richard Nixon and 73 other leaders.

ULY 20, 03:15 GMT

s Neil Armstrong steps nto the Moon, he says, That's one small step for an; one giant leap for nankind." Buzz Aldrin ins Neil Armstrong nd they spend two ours exploring, taking hotographs, and collecting ock and dust samples to ake home for testing.

JULY 20, 17:54 GMT

After seven hours' rest aboard the spacecraft, the astronauts begin their journey home. They land in the Pacific.

DAWN ON JULY 24

The three astronauts arrive home four days later, in good health.

SPLASH DOWN!

A satellite is any object that orbits another object in space. An artificial satellite is one made by humans.

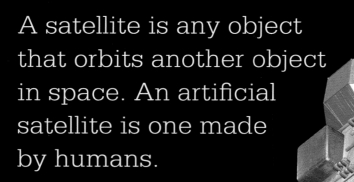

YOU CAN SEE

Just after dusk is a good time to spot satellites. They look like moving stars.

Into position

Satellites are carried into space on rockets. They are positioned so the Earth's gravity keeps them circling the Earth without drifting away.

Satellites are used in many ways.

Communication

Satellites can send television programs around the world.

Weather

Satellites watch weather and can warn people about hurricanes.

Navigation

Satellites can guide cars, ships, and aircraft, and help you if you are lost.

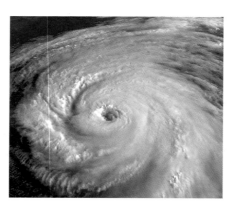

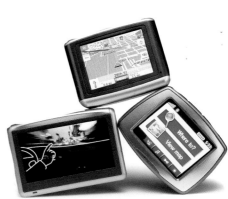

If you use satellite navigation in your car, that means

Space junk

Today there are about 3,000 useful satellites traveling around and around our Earth. There are also thought to be about 20,000 useless pieces of space garbage floating out there, too!

Space junk is bits and pieces of spacecraft that have dropped off.

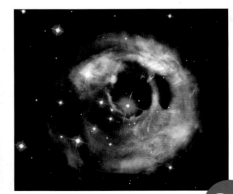

Scientists are trying to find ways to get rid of the junk that is clogging up space.

Watching Earth

Satellites take pictures of Earth, giving us information on pollution.

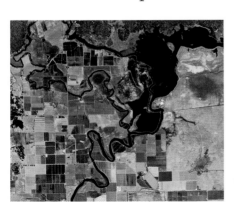

Spy satellites

Armies use satellites to watch ships and to detect missile launches.

Space discovery

Huge telescopes attached to satellites orbit the Earth to watch space.

a satellite is watching you—even through the clouds.

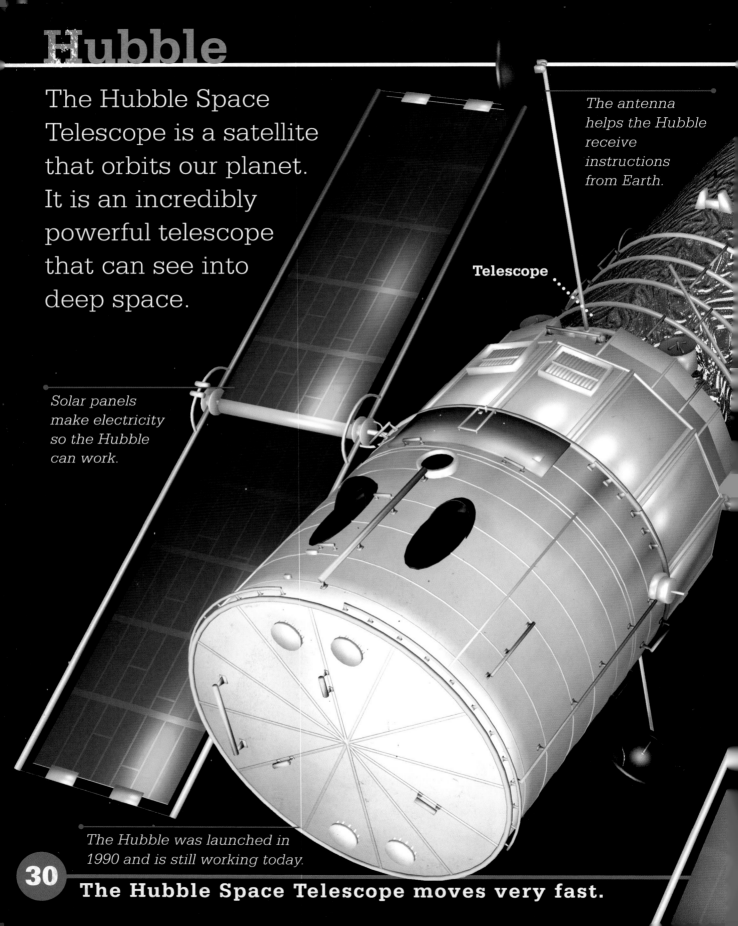

Hubble

The Hubble Space Telescope is a satellite that orbits our planet. It is an incredibly powerful telescope that can see into deep space.

The antenna helps the Hubble receive instructions from Earth.

Telescope

Solar panels make electricity so the Hubble can work.

The Hubble was launched in 1990 and is still working today.

The Hubble Space Telescope moves very fast.

The telescope has taken more than 400,000 pictures of about 25,000 objects.

The Hubble can see objects 50 times more clearly than telescopes on Earth can.

Hubble gallery

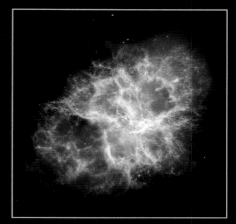

Birth of a star

Our atmosphere makes objects in space appear to twinkle. The Hubble has a much clearer view.

Discoveries

The Hubble has helped us uncover many mysteries of the universe. It has discovered black holes and distant planets.

When it needs to be fixed, the Hubble has to be mended in space. Spacewalkers fix the telescope while it is in orbit.

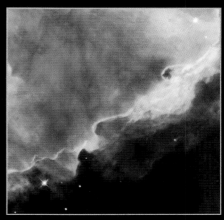

The Crab Nebula

THE HUBBLE CAN COMPLETE ONE ORBIT OF EARTH IN 97 minutes.

Death of a star

It can cross the US in about ten minutes.

Mars

Mars is known as the red planet, and although it looks red hot, it is actually very, very cold. It has valleys and volcanoes like Earth does.

4

Mars is the fourth planet from the Sun. It is the last of the rocky planets.

Discovering Mars

Since the late 1990s, robots have landed on Mars to study it. This space rover takes photographs of Mars.

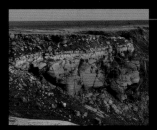

Mars has canyons, which may have once been rivers. If there was water, there may also have been life.

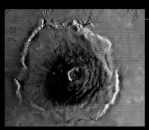

Mars has the biggest volcano ever found in space. Olympic Mons is about the size of Texas.

The Phoenix Lander *is the latest spacecraft to touch down on Mars. It has found evidence of snow falling from Mars's clouds!*

The Mars rovers are controlled by computers back on

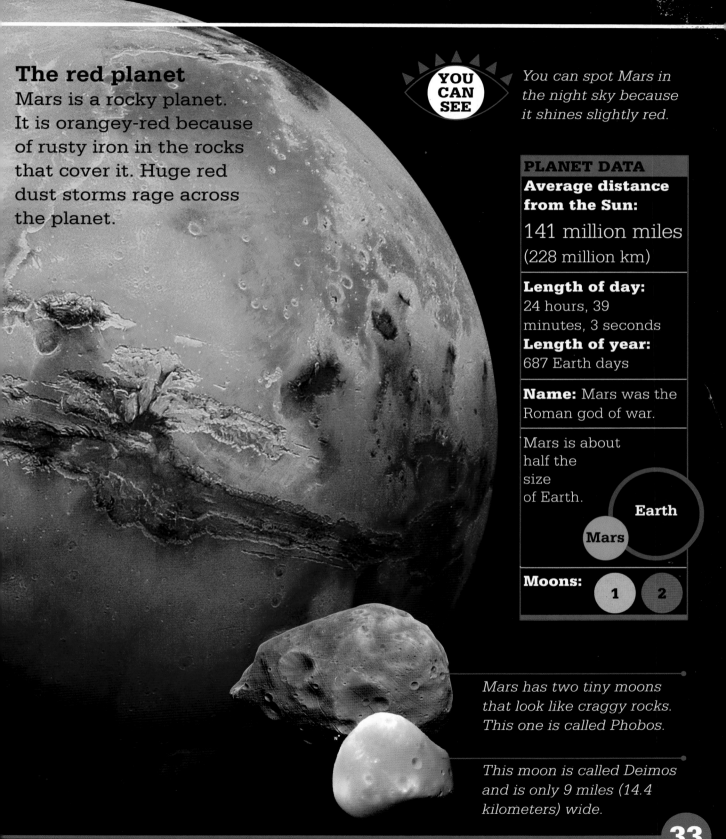

The red planet

Mars is a rocky planet. It is orangey-red because of rusty iron in the rocks that cover it. Huge red dust storms rage across the planet.

YOU CAN SEE

You can spot Mars in the night sky because it shines slightly red.

PLANET DATA

Average distance from the Sun:
141 million miles
(228 million km)

Length of day:
24 hours, 39 minutes, 3 seconds
Length of year:
687 Earth days

Name: Mars was the Roman god of war.

Mars is about half the size of Earth.

Earth

Mars

Moons: 1 2

Mars has two tiny moons that look like craggy rocks. This one is called Phobos.

This moon is called Deimos and is only 9 miles (14.4 kilometers) wide.

Earth. They record temperatures and examine rocks.

Asteroids

Rocks that float around in space are called asteroids. When they hit Earth, they are known as meteorites.

The asteroid belt

Most asteroids in our solar system exist in a ring between Mars and Jupiter known as the asteroid belt. They circle our Sun, too, just like all the planets do.

Asteroid Ida

The asteroid Ida is as long as Manhattan Island and moves within the asteroid belt. Ida has its own moon, called Dactyl.

• Dactyl

• Ida

Dinosaur death

Many people think that the dinosaurs died out as a result of an enormous meteorite hitting the Earth about 65 million years ago.

Meteorite

The Willamette meteorite, discovered in 1902, is one of the biggest ever found.

Some 99 percent of meteorites originally came from the asteroid belt.

Crashing rocks

If asteroids crash into one another, rocks are flung into open space.

Look out, Earth!

Once in a while a loose asteroid flies into Earth's atmosphere.

A giant dent

When an asteroid hits the Earth, it makes a huge crater.

Jupiter

Jupiter is the biggest planet in our solar system. It is so big that all the other planets could fit inside it, with room to spare.

PLANET NUMBER 5

Jupiter is the fifth planet from the Sun and the first of the mighty gas giants.

The gas giant

Jupiter is the first of the four gas planets. Bright yellow and red clouds swirl around it. Jupiter has no hard surface at all. In fact, if you flew to Jupiter, you would find nowhere to land.

Io
Io has more than 400 active volcanoes—some emit sulfur.

Europa
Europa is an icy world that looks like a cracked eggshell.

Ganymede
Jupiter's largest moon, Ganymede, is bigger than the planet Mercury!

Callisto
Callisto is the most cratered object in the solar system.

Jupiter's moons

Jupiter has 63 rocky moons that orbit it. The four biggest moons are the size of small planets.

If you look at Jupiter through a telescope, you can see these four moons.

The Great Red Spot

The Great Red Spot is
a giant, swirling storm
that can be seen on
the surface of Jupiter.
As the storm moves
around, it swallows
up other storms.

PLANET DATA

**Average distance
from the Sun:**
483 million miles
(777 million km)

Length of day:
9 hours, 56 minutes
Length of year:
12 Earth years

Name: Jupiter
was the king of the
Roman gods.

Jupiter is 11
times bigger
than Earth.

Jupiter

Earth ○

Moons: 63
(discovered so far)

Space probes

A space probe is a spacecraft with no one on board. It flies through space gathering information and sending it back to Earth.

Galileo space probe

Galileo was launched in 1989. It arrived at Jupiter in 1995, and for eight years it sent back exciting information about Jupiter and its moons.

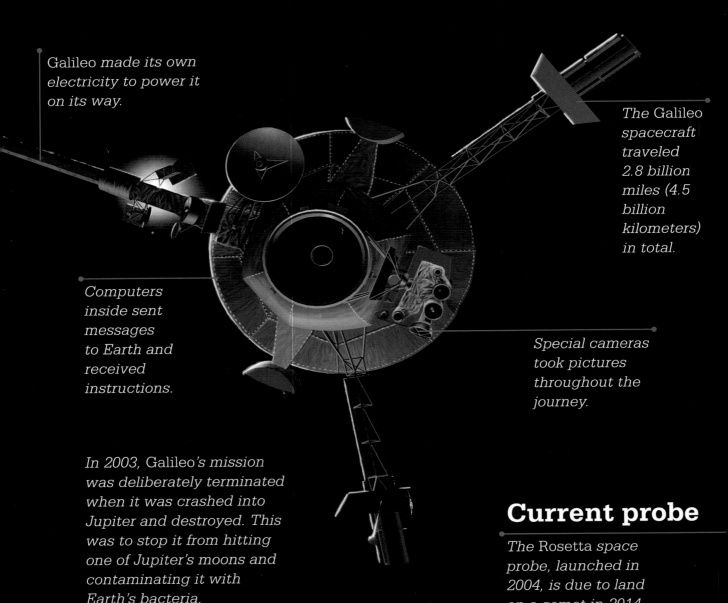

Galileo *made its own electricity to power it on its way.*

The Galileo *spacecraft traveled 2.8 billion miles (4.5 billion kilometers) in total.*

Computers inside sent messages to Earth and received instructions.

Special cameras took pictures throughout the journey.

In 2003, Galileo's mission was deliberately terminated when it was crashed into Jupiter and destroyed. This was to stop it from hitting one of Jupiter's moons and contaminating it with Earth's bacteria.

Current probe

The Rosetta space probe, launched in 2004, is due to land on a comet in 2014.

If you visit one of the space agency websites, you can

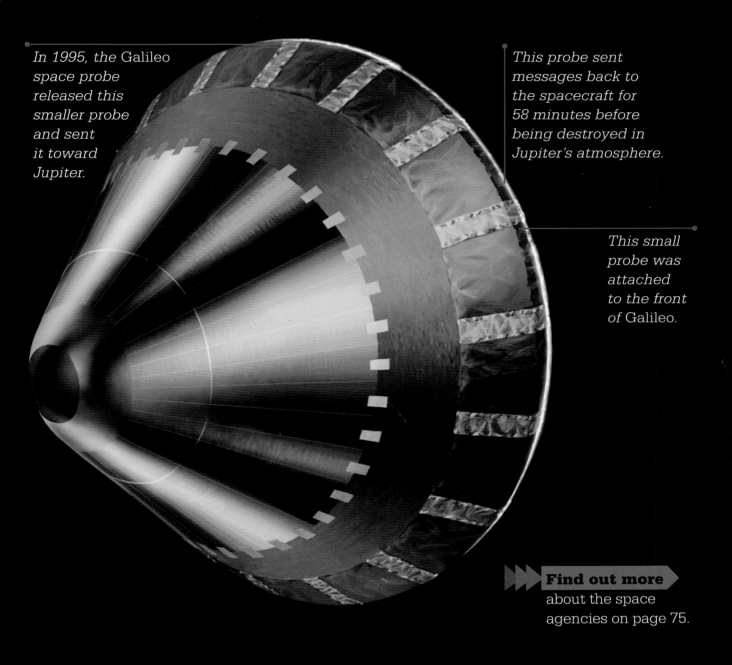

In 1995, the Galileo space probe released this smaller probe and sent it toward Jupiter.

This probe sent messages back to the spacecraft for 58 minutes before being destroyed in Jupiter's atmosphere.

This small probe was attached to the front of Galileo.

Find out more about the space agencies on page 75.

missions to monitor

The Voyager 1 space probe, launched in 1977, is heading for the edge of the solar system.

Messenger was launched in 2004 and is still traveling around Mercury.

Cassini-Huygens is a spacecraft that left Earth in 1997. It is studying Saturn and its moons.

monitor the progress of the traveling space probes.

Saturn

Saturn is a huge ball of gas that has no hard surface. It is famous for the amazing rings that surround it.

PLANET NUMBER **6**

Saturn is the sixth planet from the Sun and is very, very cold.

Saturn's rings are only about 0.5 mile (0.8 kilometer) thick, but they are 180 miles (290 kilometers) wide.

Giant eyeball

One of Saturn's moons, Mimas, looks just like a big eyeball because of the huge crater on it. This moon is small and could fit inside Texas.

If you put Saturn into a pool, it would float—it's so light

Saturn's rings

The rings of Saturn are made up of billions of pieces of ice. Some are the size of a tiny speck of dust and some are as big as a car.

Jupiter, Uranus, and Neptune also have rings, but they are not as spectacular as Saturn's.

Saturn is the farthest planet that you can see with the naked eye.

PLANET DATA

Average distance from the Sun:
890 million miles
(1.432 billion km)

Length of day:
10 hours, 39 minutes
Length of year:
29.5 Earth years

Name: Saturn was father of the king of the Roman gods.

Saturn is almost ten times bigger than Earth.

Earth   Saturn

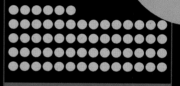

Moons: 62
●●●●●●
●●●●●●●●●●●●●●
●●●●●●●●●●●●●●
●●●●●●●●●●●●●●
●●●●●●●●●●●●●●

 Find out more
about the rings around Uranus on page 43.

Uranus

Uranus is very far away from the Sun. It is 19 times farther away from the Sun than Earth is. You can't see Uranus, or any of the planets beyond it, with the naked eye.

PLANET NUMBER 7

Uranus is the seventh planet from the Sun and is very, very far away from Earth.

The blue planet

Uranus is a giant ball of gas and liquid. The surface is made of tiny crystals of a gas called methane, which makes it look blue.

Herschel built more than 400 telescopes in his lifetime. This one, known as the Great Forty-Foot, was the biggest.

William Herschel

Uranus was the first planet to be discovered using a telescope. William Herschel spotted it on March 13, 1781.

Some scientists think that Uranus may have a rocky

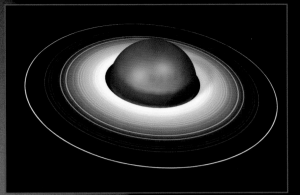

The rings

In 1977, scientists were amazed to discover that, like Saturn, Uranus has a band of rings around it.

Broken moons

Scientists think the rings could have been moons that were smashed to pieces by huge falling asteroids.

Find out more about asteroids on page 34.

PLANET DATA	
Average distance from the Sun: 1.784 billion miles (2.871 billion km)	
Length of day: 17 hours, 14 minutes **Length of year:** 84 Earth years	
Name: Uranus was the Greek god of the heavens.	

Moons: 27

Moon Miranda

Uranus has 27 moons. This one, Miranda, has dark areas that are gigantic cliffs twice as high as Mount Everest, the tallest mountain on Earth.

center, but we haven't gotten close enough to find out.

Neptune

Neptune is a giant ball of liquid and gas that lies far away in our solar system.

Neptune is the eighth and farthest planet from the Sun in our solar system.

Triton

This picture is a drawing of the surface of Triton, one of Neptune's 13 moons.

Mystery planet

Neptune was discovered when someone figured out that Uranus was being gravitationally pulled by another object, which turned out to be Neptune. It was first seen in 1846.

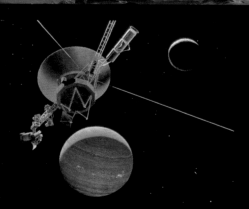

Voyager 2

The space probe *Voyager 2* flew to Uranus, then used Uranus's gravity to fling itself to Neptune. It took pictures of Neptune and is now flying into unknown space and sending back information.

Super storms

Neptune has the most violent weather in the solar system. Storms the size of Earth swirl around at huge speeds—ten times faster than our worst hurricanes.

Neptune has
1,240 mph
(2,000 kph)
winds.

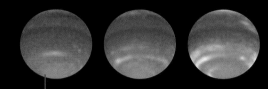

The winds are so big and violent that Neptune's surface is constantly changing.

PLANET DATA
Average distance from the Sun: 2.792 billion miles (4.494 billion km)
Length of day: 16 hours, 7 minutes **Length of year:** 165 Earth years
Name: Neptune was the Roman god of the sea.

Moons: 13

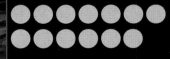

Coldest place

Triton is Neptune's biggest moon. It is the coldest place in our solar system. It is so cold that the air has frozen around it.

Beyond the planets

As you travel beyond the primary planets, there is an enormous amount of space. There are millions of icy objects there that orbit the Sun, just like the planets do.

The dwarf planet Pluto is the biggest known object in the Kuiper Belt, but it is smaller than our Moon.

Pluto has a moon called Charon. Pluto and Charon always face each other, dancing through space.

Kuiper Belt

Beyond Neptune is an area known as the Kuiper Belt. Millions of icy bits and pieces float together around the Sun.

Some people think that the objects in the Kuiper Belt are leftovers from when the planets formed.

If you travel to Pluto, take a flashlight!

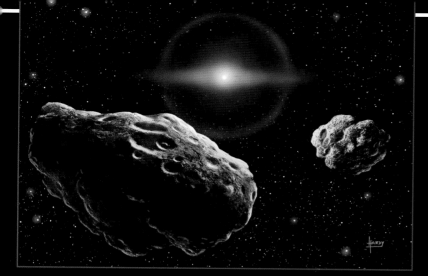

The Oort Cloud

The Oort Cloud is at the edge of our solar system. In it are the farthest objects held by our Sun's gravity. This illustration shows the Sun with the Oort Cloud around it.

Comets

Comets are balls of ice that form in the Oort Cloud. They have bright, flashing tails behind them. Comets circle the Sun, swooping toward and away from it.

Sometimes comets can be seen from Earth, like Hale-Bopp in 1997.

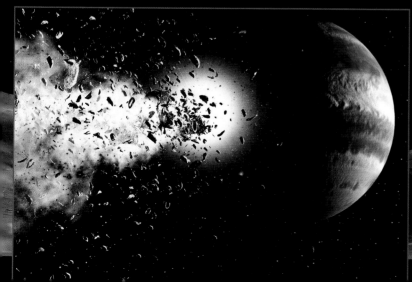

Shoemaker-Levy

In 1994, a comet called Shoemaker-Levy smashed into Jupiter. It created a ball of fire the size of Earth.

Pluto has little light.

Our solar system is part of a family
of stars called a galaxy. Our galaxy
is called the Milky Way. It is
absolutely huge. In fact, our
Sun is only one of about
100 billion stars in
the Milky Way.

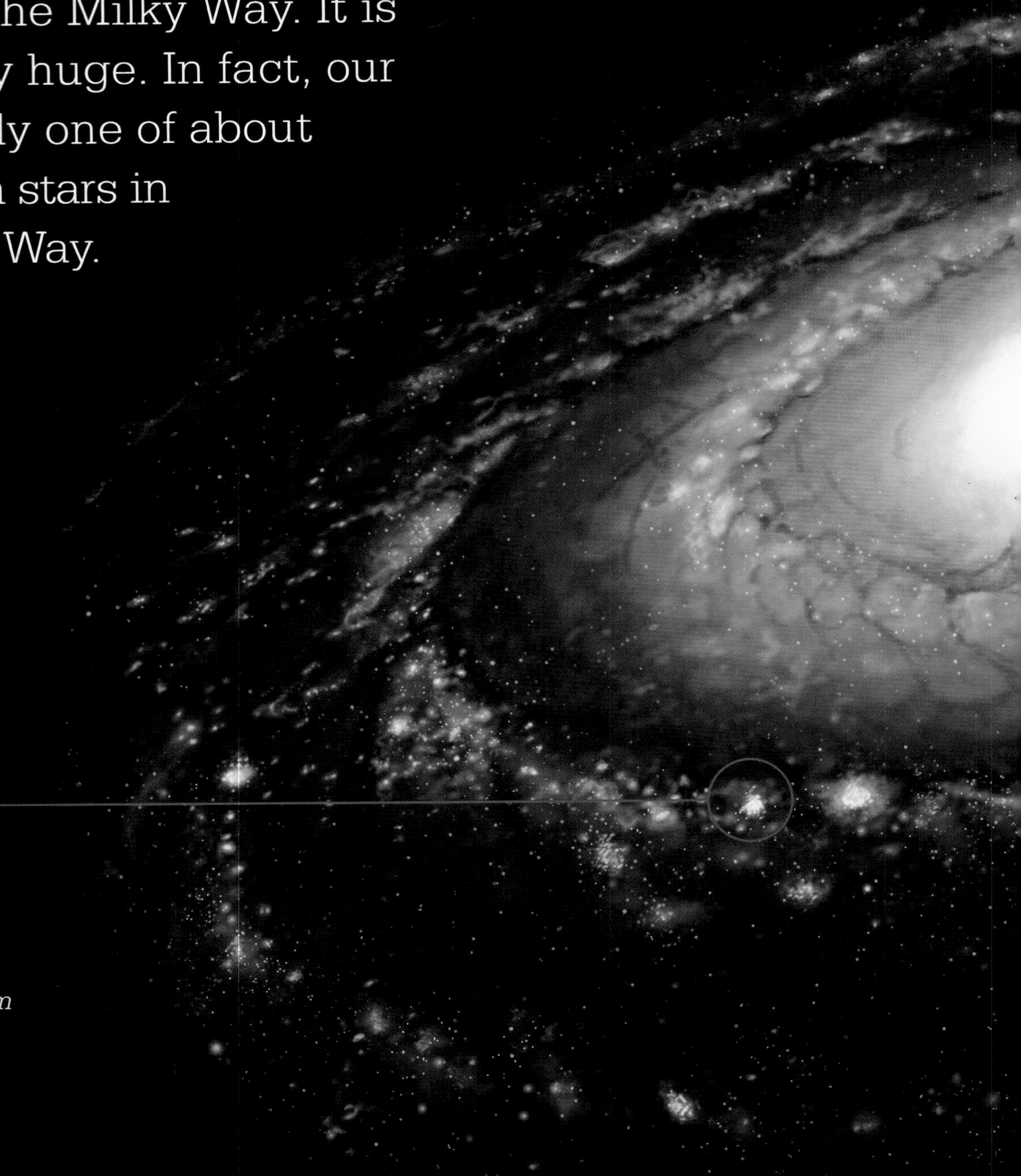

*The Milky
Way is a giant
spiral of stars
with arms that
curve outward.
Our solar system
lives in one of
the arms.*

Our solar system travels in space. It takes 250 million

Galaxy spotting

The Milky Way is shaped like a pancake—from the side, it looks like a flat line. You can sometimes see its shape in the sky. All the stars we see are in the Milky Way.

YOU CAN SEE

years for it to make one revolution of our galaxy.

Stars

Beyond our solar system are billions of stars. Some are just like our Sun, and some are much bigger.

Star birth

Stars begin life in swirling clouds of gas and dust called nebulae. Everything mixes into a ball that heats up and gets bigger and bigger.

Star death

When a star dies, sometimes it shrinks into a tiny point in space—like water going down a drain. This is called a black hole.

Galaxies

Our Milky Way isn't the only galaxy in the universe. There are millions of others. There are three main types: spiral, irregular, and elliptical (egg-shaped).

The Andromeda Galaxy is spiral.

The Magellanic Cloud is irregular.

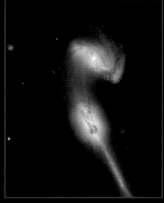
The Mice Galaxies are elliptic.

Cosmic crash!

Most galaxies are millions of miles away from us, but the Hubble telescope spotted these two galaxies bumping into each other.

These galaxies are 500 light-years away from Earth.

Our Sun is a medium-size star. The superstar Antares is 800 times wider than our Sun.

Extrasolar planets

Astronomers have always wondered whether there are other planets orbiting distant stars. Recently they have started to make some exciting discoveries.

More than 500 planets have been discovered so far. Scientists think there could be billions in our galaxy.

Most extrasolar planets seen so far are gas, like Jupiter, but one or two have been found that are made of rock, like our planet Earth.

Life in the skies

A boiling-hot extrasolar planet has shown signs of having water on it—perhaps that means that creatures live there!

It's exciting to think that there might be planets like

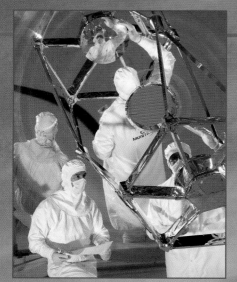

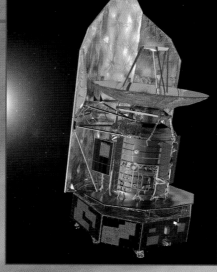

Faraway planets

In the last few years, observatories, such as Herschel, have started to spot extrasolar planets. Like the planets in our solar system, they orbit stars, and could be made of gas or liquid.

The Herschel Space Observatory, built by the European Space Agency and launched in 2009, is the biggest infrared telescope in space.

Herschel orbits Earth. It collects infrared radiation from some of the coldest and most distant objects in the known universe.

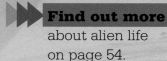

Find out more about alien life on page 54.

Earth somewhere out there in space, perhaps with life.

Is anyone out there?

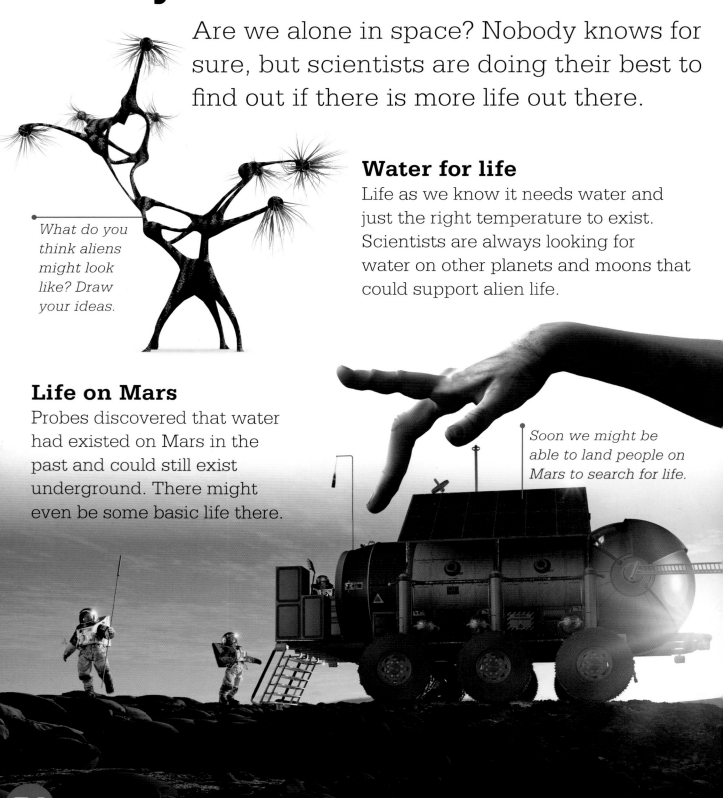

Are we alone in space? Nobody knows for sure, but scientists are doing their best to find out if there is more life out there.

What do you think aliens might look like? Draw your ideas.

Water for life

Life as we know it needs water and just the right temperature to exist. Scientists are always looking for water on other planets and moons that could support alien life.

Life on Mars

Probes discovered that water had existed on Mars in the past and could still exist underground. There might even be some basic life there.

Soon we might be able to land people on Mars to search for life.

There are many ideas about what aliens might look like. This is just one idea.

Life on other planets

The Hubble has discovered that this extrasolar planet has the gas carbon dioxide in its atmosphere, which is vital for plants. Could there be life and plants on another planet besides Earth?

Messages from Earth

The *Voyager* space probes carry messages and photographs of Earth on board, just in case alien life encounters them.

Find out more about extrasolar planets on page 52.

Look up at the sky on a clear night and it may seem like just a mass of stars. But get to know the stars and you will start to see patterns.

Find out when planets can be easily seen from Earth, and see if you can spot them.

YOU CAN SEE

Venus

Mars

Saturn

Spotting planets

If you watch the sky at night, you will see that the stars appear to move across the sky together. But the planets have their own paths.

Thousands of years ago, people used star positions at

The Big Dipper

In the northern hemisphere, the Big Dipper is an easy pattern to spot.

The Southern Cross

In the southern hemisphere, you can see this cross shape in the sky.

At certain times of the year, asteroids arrive in clusters known as meteor showers.

Shooting stars

Stars that appear to shoot across the sky are in actual fact asteroids entering our atmosphere and burning up.

night to direct them when they sailed across oceans.

Observatories

An observatory is a place where we can watch space. The night sky can be seen very clearly from a few places on Earth.

Telescopes
Most telescopes look into space using mirrors and dishes. Others pick up sound waves and infrared radiation.

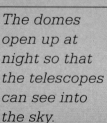

The domes open up at night so that the telescopes can see into the sky.

Observatories are often sited at high altitudes to get

Each of the buildings has a telescope inside.

Mauna Kea

Mauna Kea Observatory in Hawaii is very high up, so it has a clear view of space. In fact, it is 13 observatories run by 11 different countries.

The telescopes can see clearly in Hawaii because they are above the clouds.

Some of the mirrors used to see into space are 33 feet (10 meters) wide.

Find out more about infrared on page 53.

Rockets

All spacecraft, such as
satellites, are blasted away
from the Earth using rockets.

Ariane 5

*The Ariane
rockets are
used to take
satellites
into space.*

*The satellites
are carried
inside the
nose cone.*

*These two
rocket
boosters
blast the
Ariane
into space.*

*The Ariane
rocket does
its job only
once. It is
then left
to drift
in space.*

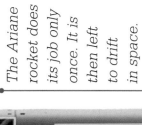

1. The satellite

This weather satellite
is checked and placed
inside a rocket.

2. To the pad

The rocket is towed
on railway tracks to
the launchpad.

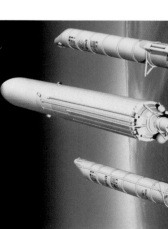

3. The launch

When everything has been checked, the rocket blasts off. About a minute after liftoff, the rocket is moving as fast as a bullet.

4. Booster drop

The two rocket launchers, or boosters, attached to the sides have done their job lifting the rocket off the ground. They fall away into the ocean below.

5. Opening up

The rocket now powers itself. The nose cone drops away and the satellites can be seen.

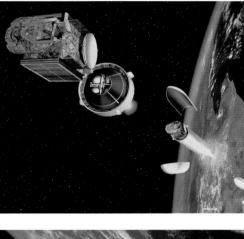

6. Satellites away

The rocket releases the satellites into orbit. The rocket has then done its job and drifts away.

10, 9, 8, 7, 6, 5, 4, 3, 2, 1 . . . LIFTOFF!

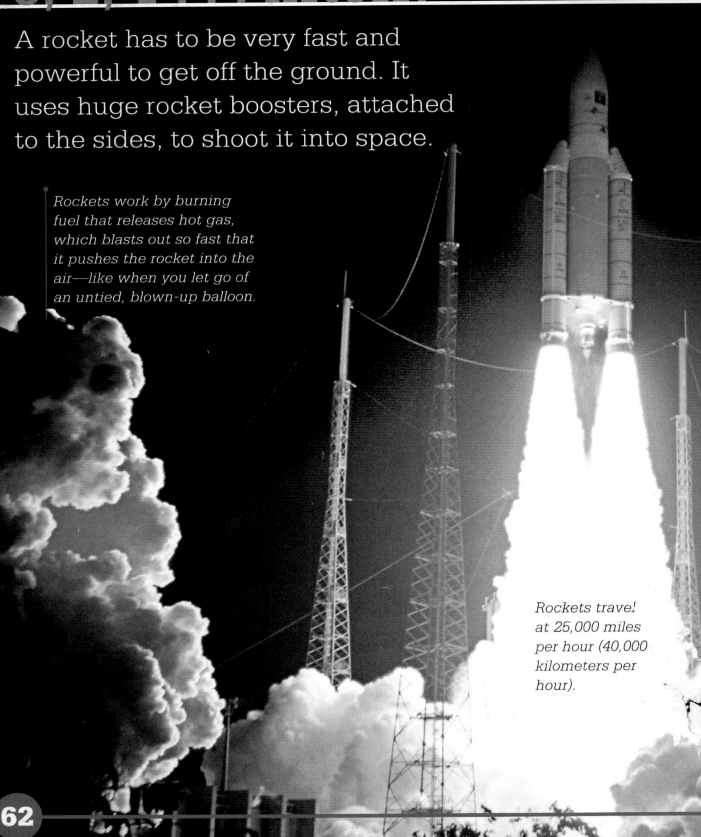

3, 2, 1 . . . liftoff!

A rocket has to be very fast and powerful to get off the ground. It uses huge rocket boosters, attached to the sides, to shoot it into space.

Rockets work by burning fuel that releases hot gas, which blasts out so fast that it pushes the rocket into the air—like when you let go of an untied, blown-up balloon.

Rockets travel at 25,000 miles per hour (40,000 kilometers per hour).

Countdown

About a minute before launch, everything has to be checked, including the weather. When everything is perfect, the countdown can begin. The final countdown tells everyone when to do their jobs.

On Earth, mission control monitors every movement of the rocket.

Flight controllers are in contact with the crew twenty-four hours a day.

A space shuttle is a spacecraft that can carry people into space. It then returns to Earth again, just like an airplane does.

3. The shuttle uses fuel stored in the orange tank to fly into space.

1. At liftoff, the rocket boosters explode into flames and force the shuttle into the air.

2. Soon after liftoff, the rocket boosters fall away and parachute into the sea.

It takes 8½ minutes for the space shuttle to reach space.

▶▶▶ **Find out more** about living in space on page 70.

The shuttle can carry up

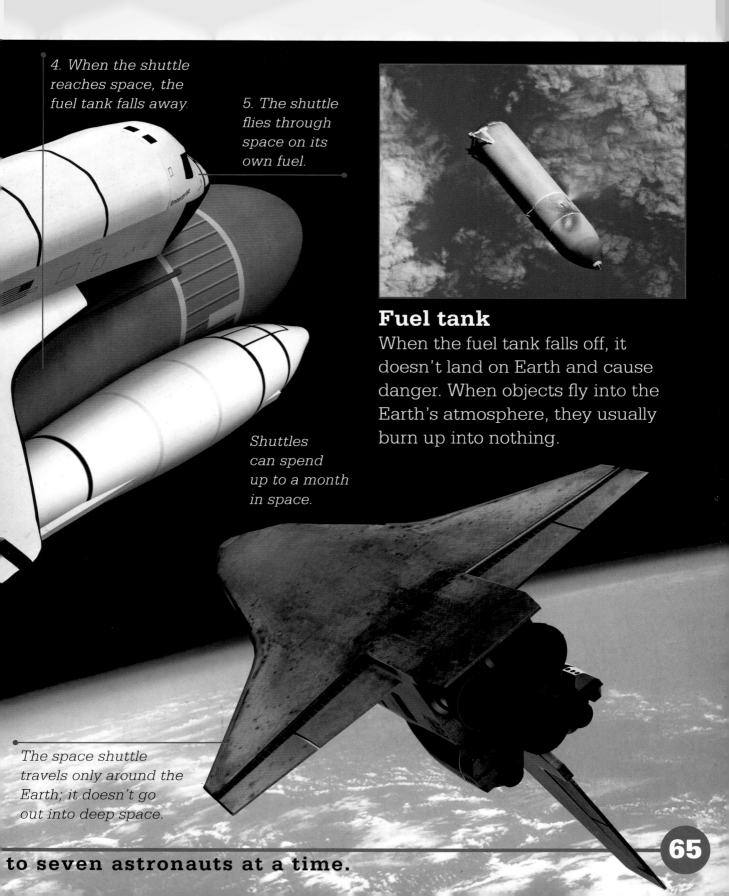

4. When the shuttle reaches space, the fuel tank falls away.

5. The shuttle flies through space on its own fuel.

Fuel tank

When the fuel tank falls off, it doesn't land on Earth and cause danger. When objects fly into the Earth's atmosphere, they usually burn up into nothing.

Shuttles can spend up to a month in space.

The space shuttle travels only around the Earth; it doesn't go out into deep space.

to seven astronauts at a time.

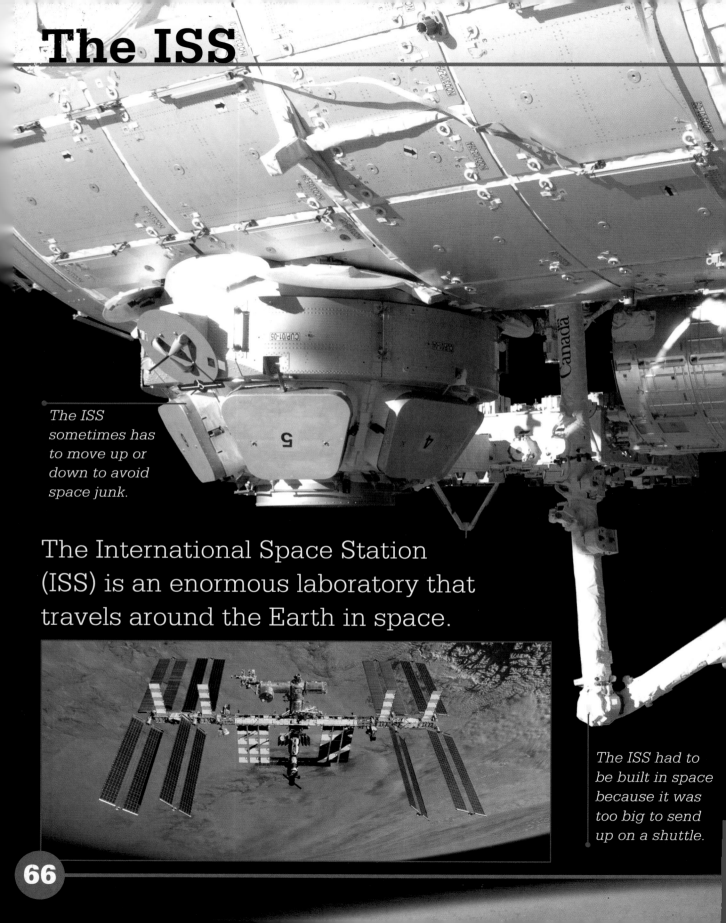

The ISS

The ISS sometimes has to move up or down to avoid space junk.

The International Space Station (ISS) is an enormous laboratory that travels around the Earth in space.

The ISS had to be built in space because it was too big to send up on a shuttle.

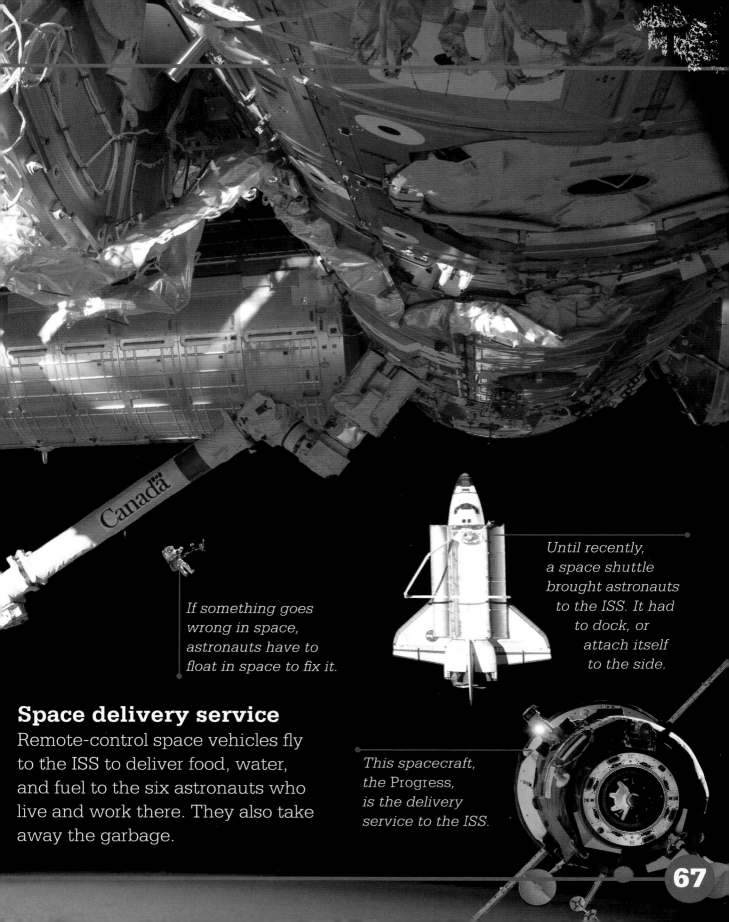

If something goes wrong in space, astronauts have to float in space to fix it.

Until recently, a space shuttle brought astronauts to the ISS. It had to dock, or attach itself to the side.

Space delivery service

Remote-control space vehicles fly to the ISS to deliver food, water, and fuel to the six astronauts who live and work there. They also take away the garbage.

This spacecraft, the Progress, *is the delivery service to the ISS.*

The space suit

Astronauts have to wear space suits when they are outside a spacecraft or space station. Space suits provide food, water, air, and even electric power.

The helmet protects the astronaut's head from small objects that might hit it in space.

The visor is lined with gold for protection from the Sun's rays.

Inside the suit is a pouch filled with water. The astronaut bites a tube near his or her mouth to have a drink.

If an astronaut floats away, he or she can use thrusters—little rockets on his or her back—to fly back to safety.

The space suit is made up of fourteen layers. Some layers protect from heat or cold. One is fire resistant, one is waterproof, and one is even bulletproof to protect from flying objects.

Getting in and out of the space suit is time consuming, so astronauts wear adult diapers instead of using a toilet.

The gloves are heated at the fingertips to keep hands warm.

Space suits can be attached to spacecraft using rings and cords that stop the astronaut from floating away.

A wristband holds a checklist of jobs that the astronaut will do on the space walk.

Astronauts wear special underwear, with tiny tubes of water running through it, to protect from overheating or freezing.

A day in the ISS

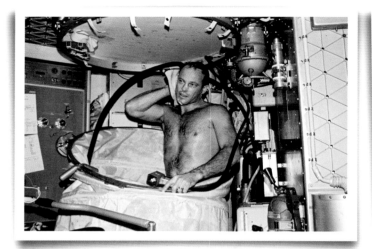

Wake up!
Everything floats away in the space station—and that includes water, so no baths. Astronauts begin their day by using a damp sponge to wash.

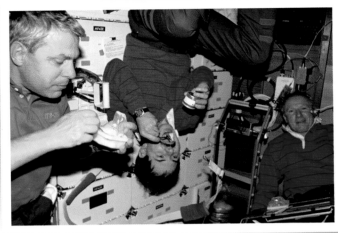

Mealtime
Astronauts eat three times a day. Their food is kept in special packages to keep it from flying away. Spacecraft from Earth deliver the food regularly.

Going to work
Astronauts do experiments in space that can help us on Earth. They grow plants for medicines and test fuels that might create less pollution.

Toilet time
Water floats around like big bubbles— urine does, too! When astronauts use the toilet, the waste is sucked away by a machine that is like a vacuum cleaner.

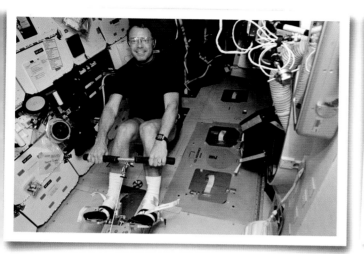

Space workout

At least two hours each day are spent on exercise. It is important to keep the crew fit and healthy, as bones and muscles become weak in space.

Doing the housework

The ISS is like a large house that needs lots of care and attention. Much time is spent on housework, such as cleaning, and everyone helps.

Space walk

The ISS had to be made in space because it is so big. Can you imagine building a spacecraft while wearing a space suit and floating around?

Time for bed

Astronauts have to attach themselves to something when they sleep so they don't float away! They climb into sleeping bags fastened to the wall.

Interview

Name: Andreas Mogensen
Nationality: Danish
Profession: ESA Astronaut

Q What does it feel like to be weightless?

A Imagine the floor disappearing beneath your feet, but instead of falling you stay in the air. It is very calm and is probably the closest we can come to flying like a bird.

Q Is it true that some astronauts feel sick when they are weightless?

A Many astronauts feel sick but there are medicines nowadays that can help those that do feel sick.

Q Does space food taste good?

A Space food tastes surprisingly good! A good meal can relax us and make us feel better, so a lot of effort goes into making the food taste nice.

Q Is a spacesuit heavy?

A On Earth, the space suit is very heavy to wear—about 300 pounds (136 kg), the weight of two men. But in space it weighs nothing because everything is weightless. It is, however, quite stiff to move in, so it takes a lot of strength to bend our arms and legs.

Q What languages do astronauts speak to one another in?

A On the ISS, the astronauts speak either English or Russian. All astronauts must speak these two languages.

with an astronaut

Q **Why do astronauts have to train underwater?**

A Astronauts need to learn how to work without gravity before going into space. When you float in water, it feels a bit like floating in space, so it is a good place to practice.

Q **Do you know how to fly an airplane?**

A All astronauts have to do flight training. To fly a plane you have to learn to control it while reading the instruments and talking on the radio, all at the same time. This helps to prepare an astronaut for work in space.

Q **What other training do you have to do?**

A As well as lots of other science and space training, it is very important that astronauts can work together as a team and get along with each other. We were sent into the wilderness for a week and had to find our food and build shelters together.

Q **Now that the space shuttle will no longer fly, how will you travel to space?**

A The Russian Soyuz rocket will ferry all the astronauts to and from the ISS. It is a three-person capsule without wings that launches and lands in Kazakhstan, Asia.

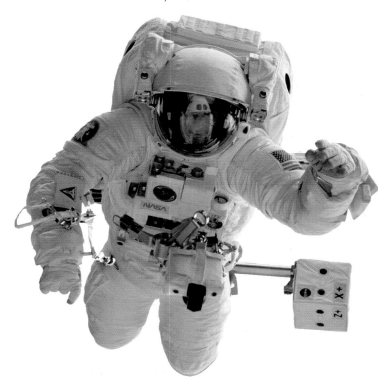

Q **What do you think will be the next big step in space discovery?**

A Mars is the next step in space exploration. Perhaps we can find signs of life on Mars.

Space—the future

In the past 50 years, we have learned so much about space, but there is a lot more to find out. What is beyond our solar system? Is there life on other planets? The future is incredibly exciting.

Humans in space

The next big plans for space exploration are to fly astronauts to Mars and to build a space station on the Moon. Perhaps we will be taking vacations in space, too!

Space inventors often make things that we end up

Bar codes

Bar codes were invented to keep a log of the millions of parts used to make space vehicles.

Eye tests

NASA scientists adapted space optics technology into a simple new eye screening test.

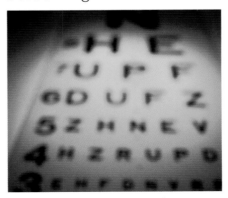

Ski boots

The folding buckles on ski boots were invented for astronauts.

NASA and ESA have great websites for kids. Look them

Space agencies

The National Aeronautics and Space Administration (NASA), the US space agency, is one of many around the world that work to discover more about our universe.

ESA *European Space Agency*

FKA/RKA *Russian Federal Space Agency*

JAXA *Japan Aerospace Exploration Agency*

CSA *Canadian Space Agency*

The space agencies often work together to train astronauts and fund space exploration.

using on Earth, too. These are some space spin-offs.

Ear thermometers

The heat sensor used in thermometers was first invented to discover the birth of new stars.

Cordless tools

Cordless tools were originally invented to drill rocks on the Moon—where there are no electrical outlets.

Fire suits

Some firefighter suits are actually fire-resistant space suits.

up and see what's going on in space.

Glossary

Asteroid
A rock that floats in space, orbiting the Sun.

Astronaut
A person who has been trained to travel and work in a spacecraft.

Atmosphere
The mixture of gases that surrounds a planet.

Black hole
An area in space where gravity is so strong that nothing can escape it, not even light.

Comet
A ball of ice and dust that orbits the Sun.

Constellation
A group of stars that forms a shape or figure. Many were named by the ancient Greeks after animals, objects, or mythological heroes.

Crater
A dent caused by an explosion or an impact by an object such as an asteroid.

Eclipse
What occurs when a planet or moon covers the Sun and stops sunlight from passing. A solar eclipse happens when the Moon completely covers the Sun, blocking sunlight from reaching Earth.

Extrasolar
Beyond the solar system.

Galaxy
A group of stars. There are billions of galaxies in the universe, and there are three main types: spiral, irregular, and elliptical (egg-shaped).

Gravity
The force that attracts objects toward one another. It is also the force that attracts, or pulls, objects toward the Earth.

Infrared
Invisible wavelengths just beyond red in the visible spectrum.

Kuiper Belt
A region in the solar system beyond the orbit of Neptune that contains millions of icy particles.

Light-year
The distance that light travels in one year.

Lunar
Relating to the Moon.

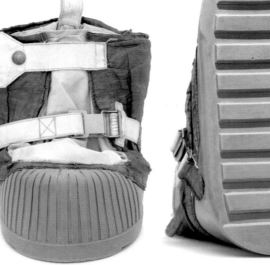

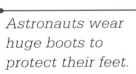

Astronauts wear huge boots to protect their feet.

Meteorite
A rock that falls to Earth's surface from space.

Milky Way
The galaxy that includes the Sun and the eight primary planets, including Earth. The Milky Way is our galaxy. Our solar system exists in one of the arms of the galaxy.

Moon
Earth's only natural satellite. It orbits Earth and is Earth's closest neighbor.

Nebula
A cloud of gas and dust in space.

Observatory
A specially designed building that has telescopes and other instruments for studying the stars and the weather.

Oort Cloud
Comets orbiting the Sun at the extreme edge of the solar system.

Orbit
To circle around a planet or star. An orbit is also the journey through space that an object takes around a planet or star.

Planet
A round object that orbits a star. It is either rocky or made up of gases. There are eight primary planets in our solar system. Earth is one of these planets.

Revolve
To keep turning in a circle or orbit around a central point or object.

Rocket
A vehicle that is propelled by engines and is designed for traveling through space.

Rotate
To move in a circle around a central point.

Satellite
An object that orbits a planet. The Moon is a natural satellite that orbits Earth. A human-made satellite can be placed in space to orbit a planet in order to collect information.

Solar
Relating to the Sun.

Solar flare
A sudden eruption of energy on or near the surface of the Sun. Solar flares can disrupt radio communications on Earth.

Solar system
The stars, planets, moons, asteroids, comets, and other objects orbiting the Sun. The Sun is at the center of the solar system.

Spacecraft
A vehicle that travels into space.

Space probe
A spacecraft that travels into space without people on board. It is used to collect information about space.

Space shuttle
A spacecraft that travels into space with people on board.

Star
An object made of burning gas. A star shines with light and may be seen in the sky.

Sun
A huge ball of hot, fiery gas. The Sun is a star in our solar system.

Universe
Everything that exists. It is the entirety of space, including all the planets and stars.

Index

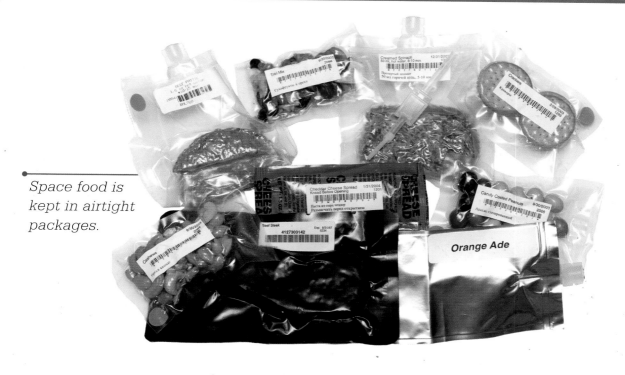

Space food is kept in airtight packages.

Thank you